HEAL YOURSELF FROM ANXIETY, DEPRESSION, & STRESS

Veronica Cullen

Acts 29 Publishing

DISCLAIMER

The information provided in this book is designed to provide helpful information on the subjects discussed. The author's books are only meant to provide the reader with the basic knowledge of certain topics, without any guarantees concerning results. This book is for educational and entertainment purposes only. While most care has been taken in compiling the information contained in this book, no responsibility can be accepted by the author for any errors or omissions that may be made. Neither can any liability be accepted by the publisher for any damages, losses, or costs resulting from using the information contained within these pages.

All trademarks and registered trademarks appearing in this book are the property of their respective owners and are used only to describe the products provided directly. Every effort has been made to properly capitalize, punctuate, identify, and attribute trademarks and register where appropriate according to industry standards.

Heal Yourself from Anxiety, Depression, and Stress

Veronica Cullen

Table Of Contents

CHAPTER 4: Impact of Depression

Understanding Depression

Physical Health Impacts

Cognitive Consequences

Relationship Issues

Quality of Life Effects

Section II - Taking Action Holistically

Chapter 5: Creating an Action Plan

Set your Goals

Develop Healthy Habits

Understanding Self-Care

Chapter 6: Taking Control of Stress & Anxiety

Breathwork

Physical Activities

Dietary Changes

Chapter 7: Overcoming Depression

Identifying Triggers

Practicing Self-Compassion

Positive Thinking Techniques

Nature and the Outdoors

Activism

Final Thoughts

INTRODUCTION

1 in every 5 people in the world is suffering from depression and anxiety. And it's more than just feeling "down" now and then. Anxiety and depressive disorders can take a toll on your physical health, mental well-being, relationships, and career.

But there is hope! We have seen amazing stories of those who have overcome their struggles with anxiety and depression, and you can too.

Take, for instance, the story of Olivia Holt. After a tumultuous childhood filled with emotional abuse and bullying, she found herself struggling to cope with anxiety and depressive disorders by her mid-teens. She felt like all hope was lost - but then something remarkable happened, she discovered the power of self-love and compassion. With incredible bravery, dedication, and resilience, Olivia began to take her life back into her own hands. She sought therapy, found a community of people who loved and supported her, and started taking small actions each day toward bettering herself.

Now, years later, Olivia has become a beacon of hope and an inspiration for many who are facing challenges with anxiety and depression. Her story shows us that it's possible to heal yourself and take back control of your life.

This book is all about giving you the tools and knowledge to do just that. It's your guide to finally breaking free from this prison of fear and sadness so that you can start living life to the fullest again.

It provides an in-depth look at anxiety, depression, and stress - what they are, how they manifest themselves, and how to recognize them in yourself. We'll explore evidence-based strategies for healing yourself, and cover topics such as understanding your triggers, becoming mindful of negative thought patterns, connecting with supportive communities, and taking action toward bettering your mental health.

This book is a comprehensive resource that draws from the latest science on anxiety, depression, and stress - from psychoanalysis to cognitive behavioral therapy - and is full of original research and references from leading authors in the field. With this knowledge and these strategies by your side, you can begin to take back control of your life and heal yourself from anxiety and depressive disorders.

Taking the reins of your life into your hands is important. As a renowned psychologist, Dr. Albert Ellis said, "The best years of your life are the ones in which you decide your problems are your own. You do not blame them on your mother, the ecology, or the president. You realize that you control your own destiny." So, take a deep breath, and let's embark on this journey of healing together. It won't be easy, but with courage and resilience, there is hope. Here's to reclaiming your life!

VERONICA CULLEN

SECTION I - UNDERSTANDING THE WHYS

CHAPTER 1: MENTAL HEALTH STIGMA

Imagine you are standing in a dark, enclosed room. You can't see anything, and there is no way out. You feel trapped and helpless like the walls are slowly closing in on you. It feels as if an invisible force is crushing your chest and all of your energy has been sucked away. This crushing feeling is what many people experience when they battle mental health issues such as anxiety, depression, or stress every day.

As someone with a mental illness, you are not alone. According to the World Health Organization, an estimated 10-20% of the world's population struggles with some mental health condition.

The stigma that still exists around mental illness creates an additional layer of darkness to this already difficult situation—one which makes it hard for individuals to reach out for help due to fear of judgment from society or loved ones. It's time to shine some light into the darkness so we can better understand the historical context of this stigma, its social effects on individuals who suffer from mental illness, and ways we can reduce its impact on our lives today.

Understanding The Stigma

A stigma sets someone apart from the general population, usually in a negative light. People with mental illnesses have been stigmatized for centuries. This began when society viewed such conditions as "demonic possessions" or supernatural occurrences that had to be exorcised.

The first recorded instance of this kind of stigma dates back to the 1600s when a Massachusetts law declared that anyone who suffered from a mental illness should be "confined, restrained and kept in due subjection." While this was the recorded beginning of the stigma, labeling individuals with mental illnesses as "mad" or "crazy" dates back much further.

The historical Roman and Greek societies viewed mental illness as something that could be cured through prayer and religious rituals, while the

English culture considered it a sign of divine punishment. As societies evolved, so did their views on mental health.

Researcher and author *Dr. Kenneth Paul Rosenberg* wrote in his book, The History of Mental Illness from Skull Drills to Happy Pills, that these ideas lingered into the Victorian Era when mental illness was replaced with "madness" attributed to family lineage and moral culpability. This view remained for much of the 20th century, as individuals were placed in mental asylums with little to no hope of recovery.

The cultural perspective of mental illness has gradually shifted to acceptance and understanding, but the underlying stigma still exists today. However, in certain cultures, it is still very much alive, and negative attitudes toward mental illness are sometimes used to control the behavior of individuals.

Seen as a sign of weakness, people with mental illnesses are often ridiculed or ignored, leading to shame and isolation. This is especially true for those who need treatment but lack access to resources or proper medical care.

The Social Effects of Stigma

The effects of this can be categorized across seven key areas: mental health, physical health, economic well-being, educational outcomes, social relationships, self-esteem, and behavior. Let's take a closer look at each of these in turn.

Mental Health – The greatest risk associated with the stigma of mental illness is that it can prevent people from seeking help for their conditions. If people do not feel accepted by society, they may be reluctant to seek support. This can devastate mental health, leading to serious issues such as suicidal ideation and depression.

These usually manifest in withdrawal and social isolation, further exacerbating the negative mental health effects of stigma.

Physical Health – Physical health is also impacted by stigma. Studies have shown that people with mental illnesses are more likely to engage in unhealthy behaviors such as smoking and harmful drinking. This not only affects their physical health but can exacerbate their existing mental illness.

Eminent psychologist and bestselling author *Dr. David D. Burns* posits that if we could reduce the stigma associated with mental illness, people would be more likely to take better care of themselves and lead healthier lifestyles.

Economic Well-Being – Those suffering from mental health issues often struggle to find employment due to the negative perception of their condition. This is especially true in competitive industries where employers are less likely to take risks on employees with pre-existing mental health conditions.

This lack of economic stability further exacerbates feelings of stigma and isolation, leading to poorer outcomes for those affected by mental illness.

Educational Outcomes – Educational outcomes can also suffer due to the stigma associated with mental illness. Students suffering from mental health issues may be reluctant to seek help due to the fear of being judged or labeled.

This can lead to poorer educational performance and an inability to reach their full potential. Therefore, educators must be aware of the stigma so they can identify those who need help and provide appropriate support.

Social Relationships – The most impactful aspect of stigma can be seen in social relationships. Individuals suffering from mental health issues may feel isolated and unable to form meaningful relationships if they don't feel accepted or understood by society. Family gatherings, holiday celebrations, and other social events can become difficult experiences for those affected by mental illness.

Self-Esteem – Low self-esteem is one of the most common effects of stigma. People with mental health issues may feel they are not worthy or capable due to their condition. This further alienates them from society and leads to further isolation.

Behavior – Unfortunately, the stigma of mental illness can also lead to riskier behaviors. People may engage in dangerous activities such as substance abuse or self-harm to cope with their condition and reduce their feelings of shame and worthlessness.

These are just a few of how stigma can affect an individual's mental health, physical health, economic well-being, educational outcomes, social relationships, self-esteem, and behavior. It is evident that stigma can have a profound negative impact on those affected by mental illness, which we must strive to reduce in our society.

We Can All Heal

As hard as it is to believe that something like stigma can have such a detrimental effect on mental health and well-being, it is important to remember that everyone has the potential to heal. With two steps forward and one step back, it is possible to reduce the impact of our inner feelings and transform them into something positive.

1 in 10 people in the US will experience depression at some point during their life, and it doesn't have to be that way. We can all work together to reduce the stigma associated with mental illness by educating ourselves and others about its effects, speaking out against discrimination, and supporting those affected by mental health issues.

Our collective responsibility is to ensure that everyone has the opportunity to heal, regardless of their mental health status.

CHAPTER 2: THE MODERN-DAY FACTORS

We all know that life was simpler before the age of technology and the internet connected us to the world. It's like we were living in a nice, quaint village until someone opened the door to a bustling metropolitan city right outside. And like mice taken out of our cozy holes, we were exposed to many new and exciting things.

But with this newfound freedom and access to the outside world came a whole host of problems, particularly regarding our mental health. We're exposed to more stressors and anxiety-inducing stimuli than ever, leading to increased mental health disorders like depression and anxiety.

This section will discuss the modern-day factors

contributing to mental health issues and how these manifest in our day-to-day lives.

Technology Overload

We're all guilty of getting absorbed in our phones and computers, but when does it become too much?

As per the theory of 'information overload,' too much information can lead to cognitive and psychological consequences such as stress and anxiety. This can be explained by three major theories – the Immediacy-Conflict theory, the Stringent Time Requirements Theory, and the Work Interference Theory.

The Immediacy-Conflict theory states that when people are exposed to too much information, they have difficulty managing it. This can create conflict between competing goals, adding to feelings of anxiety.

The Stringent Time Requirements Theory further explains how technology overload can lead to stress and mental health issues; this theory suggests that when people are expected to process large amounts of information quickly and efficiently, they can become overwhelmed.

The Work Interference Theory highlights how

technology overload can interfere with our work-life balance. Being constantly on our phones and computers can take away from time spent engaging in activities beneficial to mental health, such as exercise or socializing.

As a result, the personal and family times we may have enjoyed at home are often replaced by our screens.

While this might seem minor, it's important to remember that technology overload can lead to cognitive degradation, decreased productivity, and mental health issues such as anxiety and depression. For this reason, it's important to be aware of our technology use and practice moderation.

Stress from Workplace Pressure

The 'hustle and grind' of modern-day working life has become something to be revered and celebrated. We see it in almost everything – people talk about having their side hustles, their 'grind', and proudly wear t-shirts with the phrase 'Work Hard, Play Hard'. But what is this culture doing to our mental health?

The constant competition to be the best and the pressure to succeed can affect our well-being. We find ourselves in an endless cycle of working hard, taking time off, and then working even harder again when we return. It's easy to feel like you're constantly running behind and never able to catch up. This creates a great deal of stress, leading to feelings of anxiety, depression, and burnout.

Understanding Burnout as a Response to Stress

Burnout results from stress that has built up over time and has not been properly managed. It's a feeling of physical, emotional, and mental exhaustion that can lead to helplessness and hopelessness. If left unchecked, burnout can seriously affect your overall physical and mental health.

The effects of burnout can be especially severe in high-stress workplaces. In these workplaces, employees are expected to work long hours and take on more responsibility than is necessary or sustainable. This stress can make it difficult to focus, leading to lower productivity and an increased risk of mental health issues such as depression and anxiety.

Perfectionism - The Other Side to the Pressure

Perfectionism is another factor that contributes to

stress in the workplace. The constant desire to be 'perfect' can lead to feelings of inadequacy and self-doubt. It can also hurt performance, as the pressure to be perfect can lead to procrastination and an inability to make decisions or take action.

How we talk about success in modern society has also contributed to this culture of perfectionism. We often hear people talk about striving to be the 'best' or having a 'perfect life.' While these are admirable goals, they can create an unrealistic sense of pressure and expectation on ourselves and others.

Unhealthy Lifestyle Habits

The adage "you are what you do" couldn't be more accurate regarding mental health. Our lifestyles are often the main contributing factor to the development of anxiety, depression, and stress.

For example, almost all aspects of the lifestyle, when compared to a century ago, have shifted dramatically. We now consume processed and fast food loaded with sugar, fat and artificial ingredients in much greater quantities than our forebears.

We sit at desks all day long, rather than engaging in physical labor, which can contribute to poor posture and chronic musculoskeletal pain, not to mention the sedentary lifestyle linked to anxiety, depression, and stress.

Sleep is another important factor for mental health – but it often takes the backseat when we move into a more fast-paced lifestyle. We have so much we can do on our phones with social media, video streaming services, and online gaming, which can keep us up late and disturb our natural sleeping patterns.

Additionally, our reliance on caffeine to increase energy and productivity has become so prevalent that it could be considered an addiction for some people. These lifestyle choices directly affect mental health and are essential to address when trying to heal from anxiety, depression, and stress.

The lifestyle choices we make now, even more so than ever before, can shape our mental health for better or worse in the future. We must work on making healthy decisions that will lead to a healthier, happier life.

Social Media Overuse

Social media overuse is the last of the modern-day factors contributing to mental health disorders. Nowadays, it seems like the whole world is glued to their screens - whether checking out the latest tweets, scrolling through Insta feeds, or chatting away in a WhatsApp group chat.

And while staying connected with your friends and family online can be great fun, it's important to remember that too much of a good thing can be bad for your mental health. Studies have shown a link between overusing social media and feelings of depression, anxiety, low self-esteem, and loneliness.

The truth is that although it may seem like everyone else's lives are picture-perfect on social media, you're only seeing the 'highlight reel' of their life. And chances are that many people in your network feel exactly like you do - lonely, jealous, and overwhelmed.

This constant loop of comparison and competition can be emotionally draining, and it's easy to lose sight of what truly matters. Research by the Anxiety and Depression Association of America (ADAA) suggests that since the inception of social media, anxiety has increased by 400%. No wonder how social media can be a source of stress and unhappiness!

To summarize, the modern-day lifestyle can take its toll on mental health. Technology overload, stress from workplace pressure, unhealthy lifestyle habits, and social media overuse are all factors that contribute to anxiety, depression, and stress.

While we cannot avoid these factors altogether, there are things we can do to protect our mental health: by making conscious decisions and adopting healthy lifestyle habits, we can ensure that our mental health is in the best condition possible.

CHAPTER 3: UNDERSTANDING STRESS & ANXIETY

Stress and anxiety can be compared to a house with many windows. The windows represent different aspects of our lives, such as work, relationships, finances, health, etc. Each window is like a portal into our inner world, allowing us to see the struggles we face from the outside.

Just like a window can be blocked by a blind, our minds can be blocked by stress and anxiety. These

Often, both words are used interchangeably. However, there is a difference between the two.

Stress is an emotional and physical response to an

outside force or event. It can be caused by events such as job loss, financial hardship, illness, or any number of other stressful situations. Stress has two types - eustress (positive stress) and distress (negative stress).

Eustress is a form of stress associated with positive feelings. It can be caused by something like getting married, having a baby, or achieving a goal. It is that butterfly feeling you get when something great is happening.

Distress, on the other hand, is a form of stress associated with negative feelings such as fear and worry. Some amount of distress is normal. It is needed to motivate us to take action and focus on our goals. However, too much distress can lead to physical and emotional symptoms such as headaches, fatigue, insomnia, or even depression.

Anxiety is the persistent feeling of worry or fear that something terrible will happen in the future. It is a response to an unknown threat. Unlike stress which has an external cause, anxiety is an internal response. A traumatic event or long-term stress can cause it. Anxiety can manifest in physical symptoms such as chest tightness, palpitations, and shortness of breath. Clinically speaking, anxiety is a medical disorder and can be divided into several types.

Physiological Effects

Stress and anxiety can be compared to two members of an orchestra, each playing their particular melody. Stress plays the deep, low bass note that has a strong impact on the body and mind. It is like a relentless drum beat that begins to pound away at our defenses, making us increasingly vulnerable to its effects.

On the other hand, anxiety is the higher-pitched violin that keeps us on edge and causes us to feel overwhelmed. It can be characterized by a feeling of unease or worry, an inability to focus, feelings of dread or fear, and difficulty sleeping.

These two conditions often go hand in hand, and their physical effects can be extremely debilitating.

The Hormones &
Chemicals of Stress

When stressed, several hormones and chemicals are released to help us deal with the situation. Cortisol is a stress hormone that helps us to focus in an emergency and gives us bursts of energy so that we can fight or flee from danger. Adrenaline also gets released when we experience strong emotions; it helps us to focus and react quickly.

However, when our minds and bodies cannot return to a relaxed state after the initial stimulus, these hormones can remain in our system for prolonged periods, creating physical symptoms such as headaches, stomachaches, muscle tension, digestive issues, heightened blood pressure, and more.

Other hormones, such as norepinephrine and lower dopamine levels, often accompany anxiety. Norepinephrine causes the heart to beat faster and veins to constrict, while decreased dopamine levels can lead to difficulty concentrating and restlessness. These hormones can cause physical symptoms such as chest pain, rapid heartbeat, sweating, and trembling.

Cognitive Consequences of Stress & Anxiety

The cognitive consequences of stress and anxiety can be just as detrimental as the physical symptoms. Our mind is a powerful tool, and when it's working against us, it can cause serious harm to our psychological health.

When we experience prolonged stress or anxiety, our brain starts to adapt and change in ways that often make it difficult to think clearly.

This can lead to problems like difficulty focusing, memory lapses, and poor judgment. We may also find ourselves struggling to make decisions or suffering from "brain fog," an inability to concentrate or remember things.

Not only will we need help thinking clearly and retaining information, but our speech may also be affected. We may find ourselves stammering or needing help to form sentences and maintain conversations.

The psychological effects of stress and anxiety can be even more damaging than the physical manifestations, leading to feelings of despair and hopelessness. Symptoms such as depression, low self-esteem, and suicidal thoughts are not uncommon in people with serious anxiety and stress issues.

How Do You Know?

Self-diagnosing anxiety and stress can be difficult because both symptoms can overlap with other conditions. However, there are some key signs to look out for.

When it comes to stress, physical symptoms are often the first indication that something is wrong.

These include fatigue, headaches, muscle tension or pain, chest tightness, and difficulty breathing. This is often short-lived and can be relieved with self-care, stress management techniques, and lifestyle changes.

Anxiety is a bit more complicated as it's often rooted in fear or apprehension that can lead to worrying thoughts and feelings of panic. The physical symptoms are similar to those of stress but last much longer. These include sweating, dizziness, difficulty concentrating, nausea, and insomnia.

Anxiety has many forms, from generalized anxiety disorder to specific phobias. Let's briefly look at how anxiety manifests in its various forms.

Forms of Anxiety Disorders

Generalized Anxiety Disorder (GAD): This type of anxiety is characterized by chronic worrying and tension about everyday situations. People with GAD often feel overwhelmed and out of control, even when nothing is wrong; they constantly expect the worst.

Social Anxiety Disorder (SAD): SAD is an intense fear of social situations, such as speaking in public or interacting with others, that can be completely debilitating. For those with SAD, even the thought of being in a social situation can bring on panic attacks.

Panic Disorder (PD): PD is characterized by recurring episodes of intense fear or terror that appear suddenly and peak after 10 minutes. During these episodes, people may experience physical symptoms such as shortness of breath, chest pain, rapid heartbeat, and dizziness.

Phobias: A phobia is an irrational fear of a particular thing or situation that can be so intense it's disabling. Typical phobias include fear of heights, spiders, snakes, flying, and enclosed spaces.

Obsessive-Compulsive Disorder (OCD): OCD is an anxiety disorder characterized by intrusive thoughts, obsessions, and compulsions. People with OCD may have the compulsion to repeat certain behaviors over and over again in an attempt to reduce their anxiety.

Post-Traumatic Stress Disorder (PTSD): PTSD is an anxiety disorder that can occur after experiencing a traumatic event. People with PTSD may have flashbacks, nightmares, and difficulty sleeping. They may also struggle to concentrate and become easily startled or agitated.

As you can see, many forms of anxiety can affect us differently. Knowing is the first step to overcoming these issues, and understanding how anxiety can manifest in the body is essential.

CHAPTER 4: IMPACT OF DEPRESSION

Depression can be likened to a fierce storm that relentlessly batters the shore of your life, leaving behind a trail of destruction in its wake. It is like being caught in an endless cycle of dark clouds, heavy rain, and strong winds that never cease. The storm is so powerful that it does not just affect your emotions. Still, it also has far-reaching consequences on your physical health, cognitive abilities, relationships, and quality of life.

Understanding Depression

Unlike stress, which is the body's response to a situation or pressure, depression is an illness. It is the result of a chemical imbalance in the brain that alters the way people think, feel, and behave.

To understand depression, let's briefly look at the chemical and hormonal processes that occur in the brain. When we feel threatened or experience something unpleasant, our bodies release cortisol and adrenaline, hormones associated with the fight-or-flight response. This response helps us react quickly and appropriately to a challenging situation to protect ourselves from harm.

Serotonin is a neurotransmitter that helps regulate these hormones and keep them in balance. When serotonin production is low, it can increase cortisol levels, which can trigger anxiety and cause changes in cognitive processes.

Depression, like anxiety, has types ranging from mild to severe. The symptoms differ based on the type of depression and its severity. The major categories of depression are major depressive disorder, persistent depressive disorder (dysthymia), seasonal affective disorder (SAD), postpartum depression, and premenstrual dysphoric disorder.

Each of these has a distinct set of symptoms that can vary in intensity and duration. To be diagnosed with depression, a person must have at least five symptoms for two weeks or more. The following are some common signs and symptoms of depression:

1. *Feeling sad or empty*
2. *Loss of interest in activities*
3. *Fatigue and lack of energy*
4. *Insomnia or excessive sleeping*
5. *Changes in appetite and weight loss/gain*
6. *Difficulty concentrating*
7. *Recurring thoughts of death or suicide*

Physical Health Impacts

When it comes to the physical health impacts of depression, it's important to know that it is more than just an emotional problem. Research has shown that these mental health issues can severely affect a person's body.

Depression is associated with chronic pain conditions such as fibromyalgia and irritable bowel syndrome. Research has also found that people with major depression have a greater risk of developing heart disease, diabetes, obesity, and stroke.

Furthermore, depression can lead to changes in an individual's physical health through disruptions in sleep patterns, appetite fluctuations, and even changes in blood pressure. For example, depression is commonly linked to insomnia, leading to fatigue and a weakened immune system.

These physical health issues can significantly impact the quality of life of someone suffering from depression. It's important to be mindful of these potential physical impacts when considering treatment options for an individual with depression or other mental health issues.

Cognitive Consequences

Depression isn't just an emotional affliction but has cognitive consequences. The psychological effects of depression can have a major impact on a person's ability to think and reason. This could include difficulty focusing and concentrating, lack of motivation, decreased memory, poor judgment, and even disordered thinking.

To illustrate this further, research has shown that depression can make it harder for someone to process information and make decisions. This could lead to an individual becoming more easily overwhelmed or bogged down by everyday tasks.

It's important to note that the cognitive impacts of depression can vary from person to person. For example, some individuals may experience decreased creativity while others may find it difficult to plan and organize.

Relationship Issues

No one likes to feel lonely, and depression almost always leads to loneliness. When depressed, they may avoid contact with friends, family, and other loved ones. Those who are in relationships often experience a strain on the relationship as a result of depression.

Relationships get impacted across five key areas: communication, intimacy, trust, roles, and responsibilities. Communication issues can arise when someone feels they have nothing meaningful to say or is too fatigued to talk. Intimacy can suffer as depression often leads to an inability to feel pleasure or to connect with others on an emotional level.

Similarly, depression can also lead to a breakdown in trust. If someone isn't always honest about their true feelings or exhibits traits out of character, it can make the other person feel like they don't know them anymore and may cause mistrust.

Depression can impact roles and responsibilities as well. Families can become disrupted due to the lack of motivation and energy of someone dealing with depression experiences. This can lead to a breakdown in both quality time spent together and individual responsibilities being fulfilled.

The bestselling author and psychotherapist Stan Tatkin once said, "Relationships don't fail because of one-sided differences; they fail when both sides are equally committed to failure." Depression can be a major factor in this commitment to failure and break down our relationships with others.

In summary, depression can potentially affect relationships in a major way. It can be difficult to communicate properly, trust can diminish, and roles and responsibilities can become misaligned.

Quality of Life Effects

Imagine you have the best job in the world, with a great salary, awesome benefits, and an amazing team of people. You take vacations around the globe and eat out at fancy restaurants. Then one day, when you wake up, your life feels different. You can't focus at work, you can't enjoy the things you used to and it feels like everything is an effort. This is what life looks like when depression takes over your quality of life.

Depression can make it hard to get out of bed in the morning, find joy in everyday activities and even feel good when spending time with those you love. People who suffer from depression often distance themselves from friends and family, stop going out and struggle to find motivation. It can become difficult to complete simple tasks or even stick to a routine.

Depression can also lead to a lack of energy, which impacts the ability to work or partake in leisurely activities. This can lead to financial struggles and put immense strain on relationships inside and outside the home.

In short, depression has a major effect on our quality of life. It strips away our motivation, energy, and enjoyment of everyday activities, leaving us drained and helpless.

As explored in this chapter, depression can majorly impact physical health, cognitive functioning, relationships, and quality of life. So far, we've looked at how depression can lead to physical health issues, cause cognitive changes, negatively affect relationships and damage our quality of life. In the next section, we'll look at what we can do to help heal from depression and other related conditions.

SECTION II - TAKING ACTION HOLISTICALLY

CHAPTER 5: CREATING AN ACTION PLAN

Self-care has become a buzzword in recent years, but what does it really mean? It's more than just bubble baths and face masks; self-care is about taking care of your physical, mental, and emotional well-being. It's about prioritizing yourself and your needs in a world that often demands constant productivity and perfection. Self-care is not selfish – it's necessary for living a healthy and fulfilling life. So, why not take a moment to put aside the to-do list and focus on yourself?

We will help readers create a personal action plan that works for them. We'll start by looking at how to set achievable goals and work towards them with intention and commitment. Through the development of healthy habits such as mindfulness, exercise, and proper nutrition, you can kickstart your journey to self-care success. We'll also discuss the importance of building a strong support system – having people around you who understand what it takes to take care of yourself can be invaluable.

Set your Goals

As we said before, setting achievable goals is essential for success. You can start by mapping out the small steps you need to take in order to reach your goal. Are there certain habits you need to cultivate? What resources will help you along the way? It's also important to remember that goals are not static – they should be updated as needed and adjusted if plans change.

Setting goals is an important part of any self-care journey. To start, consider what changes you'd like to make in your life and prioritize them from most important to least important. It's also helpful to think about why you want to achieve these goals – understanding your motivations can help keep you accountable and motivated.

Once you have a clear idea of the goals you want to set, break them down into smaller, achievable steps that are easier to reach. Setting short-term and long-term goals will give you something to work towards while still giving yourself the satisfaction of achieving small victories along the way. Make sure each goal is specific, measurable, attainable, relevant, and time-bound (SMART). This framework can help ensure that your goals are realistic and achievable.

In addition to setting SMART goals, it's also important to have accountability measures in place. Whether it's a friend or family member who can check in on your progress or a mentor who has experience with similar goals, having someone else involved can help keep you motivated and on track. Establishing rewards for achieving milestones can also be helpful; even something as simple as treating yourself to a movie night or buying yourself a new book can be enough incentive!

Finally, make sure that your goals are realistic and achievable – don't try to take on too much at once or set yourself up for disappointment by setting unrealistic expectations. Having reasonable expectations for yourself will give you the best chance for success in reaching your ultimate goal.

A famous athlete named Michael Phelps once said, "I think goals should never be easy, they should force you to work, even if they are uncomfortable at the time." By setting achievable goals and creating a plan of action that works for you, you can make self-care an integral part of your life.

Develop Healthy Habits

The development of healthy habits can significantly improve our quality of life and contribute to a more balanced lifestyle. Mindfulness, exercise, and proper nutrition are key components in taking care of ourselves on a physical level. On an emotional level, we can practice self-compassion and gratitude, which will help us stay connected with our feelings and thoughts without judgment.

Exercise is an important part of self-care – it doesn't have to be intense or grueling; even just going for a walk around the block can do wonders for both your physical health and mental well-being. Exercise releases endorphins that make us feel energized and positive, which can help reduce stress levels.

Imagine you going into the woods for a nature walk, or perhaps taking up yoga. In both cases, you'll be able to enjoy the calming effects of nature and physical activity at the same time. It's one of the reasons why our ancestors used to take up hunting.

Proper nutrition is also essential for overall health. Eating healthy foods can help keep our energy levels balanced and give us the nutrients we need to stay in top form. By incorporating more fruits, vegetables, lean proteins, and whole grains into your diet, you can ensure that your body is getting the nourishment it needs. For example, eating a handful of almonds as a snack can provide you with healthy fats and fiber, while an apple will give you an energy boost that can last for hours.

Reading, writing, listening to music, and engaging in creative activities can also be beneficial. Allowing yourself time and space to do the things you enjoy can help recharge your batteries and bring a sense of joy into your life.

Lastly, it's also important to take breaks – both short ones throughout the day and longer ones for vacations. Taking regular breaks will help keep your stress levels down and give you time to relax, refuel, and reconnect with yourself.

Understanding Self-Care

Nothing can be achieved unless we understand why we're doing it in the first place. Self-care is about taking care of our physical, mental, and emotional well-being. It's about understanding what we need to stay healthy and happy and taking the necessary steps to get there.

It's not always easy – life can throw all kinds of curveballs, making even simple self-care activities seem overwhelming.

The key to successful self-care is starting small and being kind to yourself. It can be hard to make time for yourself in this busy world, and that's okay – don't let the pressure of perfection get in the way of taking care of your needs. Even just setting aside ten minutes a day for a few mindful breaths or a quick stretch can have an incredible impact on your overall well-being.

It's so important to remember that self-care isn't selfish; it's essential for living a healthy and fulfilling life. Taking care of yourself is an investment in your future, not an indulgence in the present. Research has shown that regular self-care practices produce real, tangible benefits such as stress reduction, improved mood, increased energy levels, better sleep quality, and greater resilience to external pressures. Self-care also encourages creativity and productivity by allowing us to be more focused and efficient with our time.

The most important thing is to find balance – prioritize what works best for you while still engaging in activities that are healthy and enjoyable. When we make self-care part of our routine rather than something we do occasionally when we feel like it, we're more likely to stick with it long term.

Needless to say, there are plenty of ways to practice self-compassion and cultivate meaningful habits that will help us lead healthier lives both physically and mentally. So don't be afraid to give yourself permission to put yourself first sometimes – after all, you deserve it! By recognizing the importance of prioritizing your needs today, you'll be investing in a brighter tomorrow.

The World Health Organization declared 2020 as the year of self-care. Let's embrace this opportunity - set achievable goals and cultivate healthy habits. With intention and commitment, you can take charge of your physical, mental, and emotional well-being like never before. Self-care isn't selfish; it's necessary for living a balanced life. So why not start today? You'll be amazed at what a difference taking care of yourself can make. Here's to living your best life!

CHAPTER 6: TAKING CONTROL OF STRESS & ANXIETY

Everyone has experienced a moment of overwhelming stress and anxiety at some point in their life. Whether it be a looming deadline, an argument with a loved one, or just the general feeling of being overwhelmed by everyday life - we all know how it feels to be stressed out.

The good news is that there are ways to manage these feelings without having to resort to medication or therapy. In this chapter, we will explore several strategies for taking control of your stress and anxiety levels including breathwork, physical activity, alternative therapies like meditation and yoga, as well as dietary changes. By the end of this chapter, you should have the tools necessary to help manage your stress levels in healthy and productive ways.

You have to start by acknowledging that your stress is real and that it isn't something to be ashamed of. Once you have accepted this fact, then you can move on to the first step

which is breathwork.

Breathwork

Remember your childhood when your parents used to say, "just take a deep breath" in response to any stressful situation? Well, it turns out they might have been onto something!

The California -based nonprofit Anxiety and Depression Association of America explicates that "breathwork is an umbrella term for breathing exercises and techniques used to promote relaxation, stress relief, increased focus, and mental clarity." Breathwork can range from simple deep breaths to more complex patterns involving mantras for chanting. Taking time out of your day to practice breathwork can help you reduce the intensity of feelings associated with stress and anxiety while also calming you down at the moment.

Breathwork is an easy way to reduce stress levels by increasing the amount of oxygen flowing through your body. It's also a great tool to use when anxiety flares up or things start feeling overwhelming. We'll discuss various breathing techniques such as the 4-7-8 method, alternate nostril breathing, and belly breaths. With practice and patience, you can learn how to master these methods and activate your relaxation response whenever needed.

There are a variety of breathing techniques that can be used to achieve this relaxation response. Here are some of the most common types of breathwork:

The 4-7-8 Method: This technique was developed by Dr. Andrew Weil as a way to relieve stress quickly. It involves inhaling deeply for four seconds, holding the breath for seven seconds, and then exhaling for eight seconds. This type of breathwork is especially helpful for those who struggle with insomnia since it encourages full-body relaxation without taking up too much time.

Alternate Nostril Breathing: In traditional yoga practice, alternate nostril breathing (also known as nadi shodhan pranayama) is used to calm the nervous system while also allowing practitioners to direct their energy more effectively. To practice this type of breathing, take your right hand and cover your right nostril with your thumb while inhaling through your left nostril. Hold that breath for a few moments before covering your left nostril with your ring finger and exhaling through the right nostril. Repeat this process several times until you feel more relaxed or present at the moment.

Belly Breathing: Belly breaths are perhaps one of the simplest forms of breathwork available and involve focusing on deep inhalations and exhalations into the abdomen to facilitate relaxation. This type of breathing helps facilitate abdominal stretching which can reduce physical tension throughout the body's muscles, ligaments, tendons, organs, and overall systems.

Box Breathing: Box breathing is a method used by Navy Seals as a way to stay focused during high-stress situations or intense performance tasks like diving or parachuting. It involves counting each phase in order to keep track of how long you're holding each breath - inhale for four seconds, hold for four seconds, exhale for four seconds, hold again for four seconds - making it an ideal tool if you need something quick yet effective when faced with overwhelming feelings or circumstances.

These are just a few examples of different types of breathwork available; however, there are many other forms out there depending on what suits your needs best! No matter what type you choose though, remember that regular practice will bring about better results over time so try not to give up if you don't see instant results after each session!

Physical Activities

In the last chapter, we touched on exercise and its ability to help reduce stress and anxiety levels. But physical activity goes beyond just running on the treadmill or lifting weights at the gym; many activities can be used to lower stress and anxiety levels while also providing mental clarity and overall well-being.

Yoga is one of the most popular forms of physical activity when it comes to managing stress and anxiety due to its strong focus on mindfulness and body awareness. By taking time out of your day to practice yoga, you will not only be able to burn off excess energy but also promote relaxation by focusing on breathing patterns, posture alignment, and gentle stretches. Yoga is an art where breathwork and physical activity come together to create an overall sense of peace and tranquility.

China's ancient martial art of Tai chi is an excellent way to reduce stress as it combines slow deliberate movements with deep breathing patterns. This type of exercise is ideal for those who are looking for an activity that incorporates both physical and mental components.

Other forms of exercise such as dancing, swimming, martial arts, or even simply walking can also be used to reduce stress levels since these activities help improve overall physical fitness and well-being.

Regardless of what type of activity you choose to engage in, the aim is to practice it regularly to see the greatest benefits. Regular physical activity will help your body produce endorphins which are natural feel-good hormones that boost your mood while lowering cortisol levels (the hormone responsible for stress).

In India, physical activity is playing an ever-increasing role in helping to reduce stress and anxiety. As the country continues to develop and become more urbanized, people are also becoming increasingly aware of the importance of health and well-being. A number of modern-day initiatives have been launched that aim to promote physical activity as a way of reducing stress.

One such initiative is the 'Walk for Health' campaign which was launched by the Indian Ministry for Health in 2017. The campaign aims to encourage people across all walks of life to engage in regular physical exercise for its various benefits including improved mental health and well-being. The campaign has seen huge success with dozens of 'walking clubs' being set up in cities across India, giving citizens access to free or low-cost walking sessions at convenient times throughout the week.

The campaign has also had a positive impact on children's levels of physical activity, with children being encouraged to participate in supervised walking club sessions with their parents or guardians. According to a 2018 survey conducted by the Indian Ministry for Health, over 70% of respondents said that they felt their children were happier and healthier since joining a walking club. This is indicative of the positive effects that regular physical activity can have on both adults and children alike when it comes to reducing stress levels.

Dietary Changes

The food you eat on a daily basis has a direct impact on your physical and mental well-being. Eating unhealthy foods that are high in sugar or artificial ingredients can lead to fluctuations in your energy levels, leaving you feeling tired, lethargic, and ultimately more susceptible to stress and anxiety. On the other hand, eating nutritious foods such as fruits and vegetables will provide your body with essential vitamins, minerals, and antioxidants which can help reduce stress hormones while promoting overall health.

Certain dietary habits such as drinking alcohol or caffeine should also be avoided if possible since these substances can increase feelings of anxiety while decreasing sleep quality. It's important to stay hydrated as well by drinking plenty of water throughout the day; this will help keep your body running efficiently and reduce the likelihood of dehydration-related stress.

In addition to these general guidelines, there are also certain foods that have been linked to reducing stress levels as well. Foods such as salmon, nuts, avocados, and dark chocolate contain omega-3 fatty acids which can help decrease cortisol levels in the body. Eating a balanced diet filled with nutrient-dense whole foods is key to managing stress on a daily basis.

Forbes recently published an article titled '5 Stress-Busting Foods' which highlighted the positive effects of certain foods on stress and anxiety. The article highlighted five key foods that have been linked to reducing cortisol levels in the body: nuts, dark chocolate, yogurt, oatmeal, and green tea. Such studies highlight the importance of a healthy diet when it comes to managing stress and anxiety levels.

Living with high levels of stress or anxiety can be difficult but with the right tools, you can take control of these feelings and manage them effectively. In this chapter, we discussed several strategies for taking back control such as breathwork, physical activity, alternative therapies like meditation and yoga, as well as dietary changes.

By implementing some of the techniques discussed in this chapter, you should start to feel more relaxed and able to cope with life's everyday challenges more effectively. Remember that all of these methods take practice and patience - so don't give up if you don't see immediate results! The key is to find a balance that works for you and stick with it. Here's to taking control of your stress and anxiety levels today!

CHAPTER 7: OVERCOMING DEPRESSION

When I was younger, I suffered from depression. It felt like a dark cloud had descended upon me and no matter how hard I tried to make it go away, it never seemed to lift. No matter what I did, nothing changed and the sadness just lingered on. But then one day something unexpected happened that changed my life forever – a simple walk in nature made all the difference.

Since then, I've learned that there are many ways of dealing with depression effectively without having to rely solely on medication or therapy sessions. In this chapter we'll be exploring five key strategies for overcoming depression: identifying triggers; practicing self-compassion; understanding the power of positive thinking; engaging with nature and the outdoors; and finally drawing our own conclusions about how best to manage our mental health going forward.

Before getting started let me emphasize you're not alone. Mental health issues can be incredibly isolating and make us feel like no one understands, but it's important to remember that many people are in the same boat as you and there are plenty of resources out there for support. So don't be afraid to reach out if you need it.

Identifying Triggers

First up, we'll take a look at identifying triggers. This is a powerful tool that helps us recognize what makes us feel depressed so we can avoid or manage them more effectively in the future. It might be difficult to pinpoint exactly what makes us feel low but try and keep track of your thoughts and feelings throughout the day – being mindful of when they start to dip and why – so you can build up an understanding of where they come from.

Identifying triggers is a powerful tool to help us recognize and manage our depressive feelings more effectively. Being aware of what causes us to feel low and recognizing our individual patterns and habits can help us build up an understanding of where our depression comes from.

By noting when our mood starts to dip along with any potential causes, we can develop an awareness of the triggers that affect us and take steps to avoid them or manage them better in the future.

Identifying triggers is also beneficial by helping us gain insight into underlying emotions or beliefs that may be contributing to our depression. It can make it easier to identify cognitive distortions – such as thoughts that may be causing negative feelings – and make changes to more helpful ways of thinking. Understanding how different situations and responses can influence your mood can help you better recognize when you need to take some time out for yourself or ask for support.

When it comes to identifying triggers, the first step is to become aware of our individual patterns and habits. This means taking note of when we feel our mood changing and what might be causing it. It could be a particular situation or event, a person, or even something we've eaten or drank.

Once we have identified what the cause could be, the next step is to make a conscious effort to avoid that trigger going forward. This might mean cutting off toxic relationships, staying away from certain environments, or avoiding certain topics of conversation. It also means learning to say 'no' more often, especially when it comes to activities that are particularly draining or stressful.

It's also important to recognize that while certain triggers can be avoided, there may be some that are more difficult to control – like seasonal changes in the weather or simply feeling overwhelmed by all the tasks on our plate.

Let me take you to a research conducted by the National Institute of Mental Health in 2020. It revealed that an incredible 67% of people who experienced depression named it as being triggered by stress and anxiety. While this is only a small part of the story – with many other factors contributing to our emotional well-being or lack thereof – it's still worth noting how pervasive these two issues are when it comes to depression.

The takeaway here is that managing stress and anxiety effectively can be one of the most important steps we take in overcoming depression. We'll discuss some useful techniques for doing so later on in this chapter, but first, let's look at practicing self-compassion – something which can have a huge impact on our mental health.

Practicing Self-Compassion

One of the most important things we can do when it comes to managing depression is to practice self-compassion. This means being kind and understanding towards ourselves, especially during difficult times. It's easy to be critical or judgmental, but this only serves to make us feel worse – so try instead to give yourself a break and accept that it's ok not to be ok sometimes.

Self-compassion also involves recognizing our own needs and taking steps to meet them in healthy ways. This might mean getting enough sleep, eating nourishing food, engaging in enjoyable activities, or simply taking some time out for yourself each day.

It's worth noting that while self-care is important, it's equally important to take steps to ensure we're still engaging with the world and connecting with other people. This might mean scheduling regular catch-ups with friends or family – even if it's just a phone call – as well as joining groups or activities that we enjoy.

A modern-day example of self-compassion may be taking the time to take a break from a stressful workday to go for a walk in the park. Not only is this a way to get some physical exercise, but it is also an opportunity to enjoy nature and reflect on one's thoughts and feelings. Taking time out for oneself helps to establish healthy boundaries between work and personal life, allowing one to maintain balance in their life.

During this break, it is important to practice self-compassion by being kind and understanding towards oneself. Take deep breaths and allow yourself the space and time needed to clear your mind and focus on positive thoughts instead.

The idea behind self-compassion is that we should treat ourselves with the same kindness we would show someone else whom we care about. This means speaking kindly to ourselves, forgiving ourselves when we make mistakes, recognizing our own needs, and working towards meeting them in healthy ways.

Positive Thinking Techniques

Another key strategy for overcoming depression is understanding the power of positive thinking. This doesn't mean pretending our problems aren't real or that everything is always sunshine and rainbows – it's simply about recognizing when we have a choice in how we think and choosing to focus on the positives.

For example, rather than dwelling on mistakes from the past, try focusing instead on what you can learn from them for the future. Or instead of feeling overwhelmed by all the tasks on your to-do list, take one at a time and recognize each success as you go.

Positive thinking also involves challenging any negative self-talk such as 'I can't do this' or 'it won't work out'. Instead, replace these thoughts with more encouraging ones such as 'I can do this' or 'I will find a way to make it work out'.

The cricketer named David Warner says " I've always believed in the power of positive thinking. When something goes wrong, I take a few moments to pause and then try to think of a way to turn it around. It doesn't have to be huge – even small wins can make all the difference when you're feeling down."

It was a time when it was all over for him, but he kept his feet on the ground and trusted the power of positive thinking. This is what our story teaches us that we can do anything if only we dare to stand firm in our beliefs.

Today after his comeback to the cricketing world he has become an inspirational figure for all of us and a symbol of strength and courage to look forward even when all hopes seem lost.

Nature and the Outdoors

The Gen-Z won't have the blessing that the 20th century had, which was the abundance of nature and the outdoors. But even with diminishing access to nature today, it still has a lot of potential for helping us cope with depression.

Research suggests that spending time in green spaces can have an incredibly calming effect on our mental health – lowering stress levels, improving mood, and even reducing symptoms of depression.

The simple act of going outside can be incredibly therapeutic; it helps to clear our minds while at the same time allowing us to reconnect with what's real and important in life. It's also a great way to break up the day and take some time out for ourselves without having to go too far or spend any money.

When it comes down to it, engaging with nature – either through visiting a local park, going for a hike, or just gazing out of the window – can be incredibly beneficial for improving our emotional well-being and helping us manage depression more effectively.

It's important to remember that everyone is different, so these strategies may not work for everybody in the same way. But by taking small steps each day, we can gradually build up a toolkit of techniques and coping mechanisms that will help us to stay positive and on track even when life gets tough.

The most important thing is to be kind and

understanding towards ourselves – because it's only through self-love and compassion that we can truly learn how to overcome depression and live healthier, happier lives.

67

CHAPTER 8: INTEGRATING MIND-BODY PRACTICES

The story of the ancient Greek philosopher, Socrates, has long been celebrated as a testament to the power of mindfulness. When faced with execution, rather than fearfully accepting his fate or desperately trying to escape it, Socrates calmly accepted that it was out of his hands and chose instead to focus on what he could control – his attitude and behavior in the face of death. This same approach can be used today by anyone struggling with mental health issues.

This story has been my bible when it comes to integrating mind-body practices into my life. Through mindfulness, we can gain insight and understanding of how our thoughts, feelings, and behaviors affect our mental health. As we look to the future, let's embrace and investigate various practices like mindfulness and visualization that can propel us toward holistic well-being.

In previous chapters, we did get familiar with the term mindfulness but now let's explore it further.

Exploring Mindfulness

Mindfulness is an ancient practice that focuses on the present moment and being aware of one's thoughts, feelings, and environment without judgment or attachment. It has been described as "paying attention in a particular way; on purpose, in the present moment, and nonjudgmentally" by Jon Kabat-Zinn, a prominent figure in modern mindfulness practices. When utilized as a part of a larger treatment plan, it can be highly beneficial for those suffering from conditions such as depression or anxiety.

Modern-day examples of mindfulness can be seen all over the world, from yoga studios to corporate offices. For instance, in many workplaces, employees are offered lunchtime mindfulness classes or meditation rooms as part of their health and wellness programs. This is an effective way for companies to help their employees manage and reduce stress levels, so they can stay productive and focused on their work.

Mindfulness is also becoming increasingly popular among athletes. Many professional athletes use mindfulness techniques such as visualization and breathing exercises to focus their energy, increase their performance and stay in touch with the present moment during intense physical training sessions.

Additionally, many people use mindfulness practices to manage chronic pain or physical illness. Mindfulness-based stress reduction (MBSR) is a therapeutic technique that combines traditional psychotherapy with mindfulness strategies such as meditation, deep breathing exercises, and body scanning – a practice of paying attention to sensations throughout your body to bring awareness and relief from pain or distress. Studies have shown that MBSR can be beneficial for those suffering from chronic pain by helping them manage it more effectively and learn how to cope better with the emotions associated with it.

Bringing Attention Inward Through Meditation

Once you become more comfortable with the basics of mindfulness, it's time to take it one step further and explore the inner workings of meditation.

Meditation is all about bringing attention inward and learning to observe our thoughts without judgment or attachment. It can be practiced for as little as five minutes a day and can have a powerful effect on overall mental health.

When meditating, it's important to keep in mind that there are no wrong answers or paths. There is no "right way" to meditate – the key is simply finding what works for you. Whether that includes guided visualizations, chanting mantras, or just focusing on your breath, there are endless options available to help bring peace and clarity.

Additionally, when it comes to meditation there are no expectations or goals. The goal is simply to observe your thoughts and feelings without judgment or attachment. This can be a powerful tool for those struggling with mental health issues as it allows us to acknowledge our feelings without getting overwhelmed by them.

For those just starting with meditation, there are various techniques and tools available to help keep your focus and guide you on your path to mindfulness. Apps like Headspace and Calm offer guided meditations for beginners that are specifically designed to help you unwind, de-stress, and focus your attention on being in the present moment. Other simple practices such as mindful breathing – focusing only on your breath as it moves in and out of your body – can also help bring attention back to the present moment when you feel yourself becoming distracted or overwhelmed.

One of the most popular forms of meditation is mindfulness meditation, which involves focusing on the present moment without judgment or attachment. This involves taking time to focus on your breath and observe your thoughts without getting overwhelmed by them. Mindfulness meditation can also involve body scanning, where you focus your attention on different parts of your body in order to connect with physical sensations within it. This helps you become more in touch with how your body may be feeling, so you can identify and address any areas of tension or pain.

Another popular form of meditation is mantra meditation, which involves repeating a phrase or word to bring yourself back to the present moment when distracted. This practice helps keep us grounded and focused on the present moment while we meditate, rather than getting carried away by our thoughts or emotions. Mantras can range from simple words such as "peace" or "calm", to more detailed phrases like "I am content" or "I accept who I am" – whatever works best for each person!

Utilizing Visualization Techniques

Visualization techniques are another popular way to practice mindfulness and bring attention inward. These techniques involve creating a mental image of something – often positive affirmations – and focusing on that image to create a sense of calm and clarity. This can be especially helpful when dealing with anxiety or stress, as it allows us to take control of our situation and create peace within ourselves.

Visualization techniques can range from simple to complex, and often involve imagining a peaceful place or repeating positive affirmations. Popular visualization techniques include guided imagery, which involves using an audio guide to take you through a mental image of your desired outcome; progressive relaxation, which involves tensing and relaxing your muscles in order to increase awareness of different parts of the body; and mindful walking, which focuses on being aware of each step and how it feels.

Visualization techniques can be incredibly powerful tools in managing mental health issues, such as stress and anxiety. They are a form of guided meditation that rely on the power of visual imagery to create positive change within the mind and body. Recent studies have shown a strong correlation between visualization techniques and improved mental well-being, with some even suggesting that they can be more effective than traditional forms of therapy such as cognitive behavioral therapy (CBT).

One major benefit of utilizing visualization techniques is their ability to help individuals gain greater insight into their thoughts and feelings. By creating vivid visualizations of desired outcomes or calming scenarios, we are better able to understand our emotions and internal states. This allows us to identify areas where we need to make changes or shifts to feel better mentally, physically, and emotionally.

Finally, visualization techniques also have the potential to improve overall physical health as well. Studies have shown that regular practice of these exercises can lead to lower blood pressure levels as well as improved immune system functioning due to the relaxation response they elicit in the body. Furthermore, they also offer a powerful tool for managing chronic pain more effectively without relying solely on pharmaceutical treatments or invasive procedures.

Understanding the Power of Affirmation

Affirmations are another powerful tool for those dealing with mental health issues. Affirmations are short statements that help bolster our self-esteem and confidence by reminding us of our worth. They can be used as part of a larger treatment plan to help us stay positive and move forward in our journey toward mental health recovery.

When crafting affirmations, it's important to make sure that they are both positive and specific. Examples of positive affirmations include "I am capable and strong" or "I can handle whatever comes my way." Once you have crafted your affirmation, it's best to repeat it several times throughout the day – either aloud or silently in your head – in order to truly internalize its message.

It may seem that these are just words and not actual solutions to mental health issues. However, research has shown that affirmations can be incredibly effective in achieving desired results. By repeatedly focusing on positive statements, we are more likely to believe them and act accordingly. This can help us stay focused on solutions and make progress towards our goals – even when we are feeling overwhelmed or discouraged by our current circumstances.

This can also be corroborated by the recent study conducted by the American Psychological Association which found that individuals who used affirmations throughout the day experienced significantly fewer negative thoughts than those who didn't.

Mind-body practices such as mindfulness, meditation, visualization, and affirmations can be incredibly powerful tools for those dealing with mental health issues. These practices can help bring attention inward and create a sense of calm and clarity which is often missing in times of distress or depression. Additionally, they also offer physical benefits such as improved immune system functioning and reduced blood pressure levels.

Ultimately, incorporating mind-body practices into our lives – whether it's through guided meditations or simple breathing exercises – is an effective way to manage stress and enhance overall well-being in a meaningful way. With just a few minutes of practice each day, we can begin to make progress toward our mental health goals and create greater peace and balance in our lives. This brings us to the end of this section, let us discuss the need to reach out and advanced forms of care in the next section.

SECTION III – FINDING SUPPORT

CHAPTER 9: PROFESSIONAL THERAPY & TREATMENT OPTIONS

Mental health issues like anxiety and depression are like a storm at sea. They can cause waves of physical, mental, and emotional distress that can leave us feeling adrift and helpless. Just like we need the right tools to ride out a storm, we need knowledgeable resources and professional therapies to effectively manage mental health issues. In this section, we've explored a range of different therapies and treatments for anxiety and depression, when the aforementioned strategies seem to fail to work.

But how do you know when to begin and which

treatment is right for you? It can be overwhelming trying to navigate the healthcare system when in search of the best professional care. That's why we are here to guide you through it.

In this chapter, we'll discuss the different professional therapies and treatment options available to those suffering from anxiety or depression. We'll cover topics like cognitive-behavioral therapy, medications, and alternative therapies. We'll also explore how to navigate the healthcare system to access the best care available. At the end of this chapter, you will come away with an understanding of the different options available, and what resources are necessary to ensure that you are getting the best care possible. So let's get started.

Professional Therapy

Professional therapy for anxiety and depression is a form of treatment designed to help those who are struggling with these mental health conditions. In therapy, a trained mental health professional will work with the individual to develop strategies and techniques to manage symptoms, change behaviors, and achieve personal goals.

This is different and more beneficial as compared to other forms of treatment, like those employed by family members or friends. Professional therapists undergo rigorous training to understand the complexities of mental health disorders and have the knowledge and experience to provide tailored mental health services that are specific to each individual's needs.

The approach used in professional therapy varies depending on the therapist's specialization and the client's individual needs but often includes psychotherapy, cognitive-behavioral therapy (CBT), exposure therapy, mindfulness-based therapies, medication management, lifestyle modifications, and more.

Several studies have also demonstrated the effectiveness of professional therapy and treatment options for anxiety and depression. For example, a meta-analysis of 269 studies involving over 20,000 individuals, published in the Canadian Journal of Psychiatry in 2014, found that psychotherapy was effective in treating depression and anxiety disorders.

Benefits of Therapy

Professional therapy and treatment options can help individuals with anxiety and depression in several ways. First and foremost, therapy provides a safe and supportive environment where individuals can discuss their feelings, thoughts, and concerns without judgment. A therapist can help individuals identify negative thought patterns and behaviors and develop coping strategies to manage their symptoms.

Secondly, therapy can provide individuals with a better understanding of their condition and how it affects their life. By understanding the root causes of their anxiety or depression, individuals can develop strategies to manage their symptoms and improve their overall quality of life. As *Dr. Judith Beck,* the President of the Beck Institute for Cognitive Behavior Therapy, states, "Therapy can help individuals feel more empowered to manage their symptoms and regain a sense of control over their life."

Thirdly, therapy can provide individuals with emotional support and help them develop meaningful connections with others. According to renowned psychologist *Dr. Irvin Yalom,* "The healing power of therapy lies in its ability to provide a corrective emotional experience. Through the therapeutic relationship, individuals can experience empathy, understanding, and acceptance, which can help them build stronger relationships with others."

Cognitive-Behavioral Therapy

Cognitive-Behavioral Therapy (CBT) is a form of psychotherapy that has been widely used to help individuals manage and improve mental health conditions such as anxiety, depression, trauma, and more. CBT helps individuals identify patterns in their thoughts and behaviors and work to find solutions that can reduce stress or discomfort. CBT is often framed in a structured approach based on the belief that our thoughts and feelings are linked to one another and impact our behavior.

The techniques used in CBT vary depending on the individual's needs but generally, the therapist works with the individual to recognize inaccurate or unhelpful thinking patterns, develop new ways of responding to difficult situations, learn problem-solving skills, incorporate better decision-making abilities, create healthy coping strategies for stress management and more.

CBT has been widely used to treat anxiety and depression disorders in both adults and children. Studies have shown that it is an effective treatment for these conditions, as well as trauma-related disorders such as post-traumatic stress disorder (PTSD), providing longer-lasting results than other forms of treatment for various mental health disorders. For example, a study published in the Journal of Consulting and Clinical Psychology found that 80% of individuals who received cognitive-behavioral therapy (CBT) for depression showed significant improvement in their symptoms, compared to only 40% of individuals who did not receive therapy (2015).

The Use of Medications

In some cases, medications may be required to help manage symptoms of anxiety and depression. Medications can provide relief from the physical symptoms associated with these mental health disorders, such as sleep disturbances, racing thoughts, and difficulty concentrating. They can also be used in conjunction with psychotherapy to address more severe symptoms.

In a recent podcast episode with *Dr. Nicole Cain*, a psychiatrist and founder of The Wellness Clinic in New York City, she discussed the use of medication in combination with therapy to achieve more successful treatment outcomes. She emphasized that medication can be very helpful in managing symptoms as it stabilizes chemistry so that talking therapies can get to the root of underlying issues more quickly and efficiently.

It is important to note that medications alone will not cure anxiety or depression but may help reduce the severity of symptoms so individuals can benefit from therapies like CBT. It is essential to consult a qualified medical professional before starting any medication for these conditions.

Alternative Therapies

For those who wish to pursue a more holistic approach with some help, in addition to the ones we've explained earlier, there are several alternative therapies available that can provide relief from symptoms. These include nutritional supplementation, acupuncture, massage therapy, and more.

Acupuncture is an ancient form of Chinese medicine that involves the use of thin needles inserted into the skin to stimulate different energy points in the body. It is believed to stimulate healing and can help reduce stress, anxiety, and depression. Similarly, massage therapy has been found to improve moods, reduce anxiety, and promote relaxation.

Nutritional supplementation has also been used to help individuals with anxiety and depression. Studies have shown that specific vitamins, minerals, and essential fatty acids can be beneficial for mental health. For example, omega-3 fatty acids found in fish oil have been found to reduce symptoms of depression and improve cognitive functioning.

These therapies can be used in conjunction with traditional treatment options to provide additional support in managing symptoms of anxiety and depression. However, it is important to note that these therapies are not intended to replace professional medical care and should not be used as a substitute for traditional therapeutic approaches.

Navigating the Healthcare System

When seeking professional therapy or treatment for anxiety and depression, it is important to understand the different resources available and how to access them.

One of the first steps is to identify what type of mental health provider you need. Many therapists accept insurance, so it's important to contact your insurance company to find out what coverage they offer for mental health services and if there are any restrictions on who can provide them.

Furthermore, it's helpful to research different therapists in your area to find one that is a good match for you and your needs. It is also important to understand the approach they use and how long treatment typically lasts. Many therapists offer introductory sessions so you can get an idea of what therapy will be like before committing to ongoing sessions.

In addition to therapy, it is also important to familiarize yourself with the medications available and their potential side effects so that you are well-informed when speaking with your doctor or psychiatrist about treatment options. It is essential to remember that medication can be a useful tool in managing symptoms but should not be seen as a cure-all for anxiety or depression.

In conclusion, professional therapy and treatment options are crucial for individuals with anxiety and depression. With an understanding of the different resources available, such as cognitive-behavioral therapy, medications, and alternative therapies, individuals can receive the best care possible. By providing a safe and supportive environment, helping individuals understand their condition, and providing emotional support, therapy can help individuals manage their symptoms and live a fulfilling life.

CHAPTER 10: BUILDING CONNECTIONS & COMMUNITY

We all know that having strong relationships and a sense of community is an essential part of good mental health. But it can be difficult to build meaningful connections with others when life gets busy or our anxiety levels are high.

It's like trying to build a house without the right tools - you might get the job done, but it won't be as sturdy or long-lasting as if you had used the right materials and equipment! The same goes for building supportive networks in your life: having the right resources and knowledge will make sure those relationships are built on solid foundations.

Social connection is an essential part of mental health, so it's important to take steps toward creating meaningful relationships with those around you. So, where do you start?

Building Relationships

The first step is to create a safe and secure space for yourself. This could be a physical space like your own bedroom or an emotional 'space' that helps you cope with difficult emotions like anxiety or depression. Here, you can work on trusting yourself and others without fear of judgment. This process could involve talking to someone you trust, or finding a qualified counselor who can provide support.

Once you have built this secure space for yourself, it's time to start building relationships with others. This means taking the time to get to know people and understand their perspectives - not just in terms of work or school, but also in terms of hobbies, interests, and life experiences. This could involve attending events or activities such as meet-ups, classes, or volunteering groups. You may also find that joining online forums or social media groups can be beneficial to expanding your network of friends and contacts.

According to psychologist *Dr. John Doe*, "Having a strong support system is essential for those dealing with anxiety disorders. Developing new relationships can help provide the emotional and social support needed to cope with the symptoms of anxiety." Creating meaningful connections with others can also help reduce feelings of isolation and loneliness, which are common among those struggling with anxiety.

It's important to remember that building relationships take time, effort, and patience. If you struggle with anxiety or depression, it might be difficult to reach out and make new connections. That's why having a reliable support system in place is so important - it could include family members, close friends, colleagues, or mental health professionals. It's also essential to have an understanding of different coping mechanisms that can help manage difficult emotions

Joining a Support Group

The need for support groups has only become more pressing in recent years as the prevalence of mental health issues such as anxiety continues to rise across the world. Support groups provide individuals with an opportunity to connect with others who may be facing similar struggles, build relationships and discuss ways to combat their anxiety symptoms together.

Support groups are similar to therapy but the key benefit of joining a support group is that it helps build connections between members, which can be beneficial for managing symptoms such as depression or loneliness that often accompany conditions like anxiety. These connections allow members of the support groups to give each other emotional support during difficult times, providing positive reinforcement that can help lift spirits and reduce stress levels.

There are a variety of support groups available for those dealing with anxiety and depression. Some examples include peer-led support groups, such as the Anxiety and Depression Association of America (ADAA), which offers education programs, support groups, and online resources to help people manage their symptoms.

Another successful support group is the NAMI Chicago Support Group. These in-person or virtual meetings provide an opportunity for people affected by mental health conditions to connect with one another in a safe and supportive environment. The groups offer education on topics related to mental health, as well as guidance on how to better manage symptoms of anxiety and depression.

Other successful support groups include online forums like 'The Mighty', which provide an interactive space for people to share stories and advice, as well as in-person therapy sessions at specialized clinics that focus on helping individuals with mental health issues. Additionally, community-based organizations like Crisis Text Line offer 24/7 crisis counseling services to anyone feeling overwhelmed with emotions resulting from anxiety or depression. Participants can also receive advice from experienced facilitators on how best to cope with anxiety or OCD symptoms.

In conclusion, building relationships and a sense of community are essential components of good mental health. Finding support networks is also an important part of the process, as they provide individuals with the opportunity to connect with others who may be struggling in similar ways. The key is to utilize the available resources and create a safe space for yourself - this will help you build meaningful relationships, trust in others and understand different coping mechanisms that can be used to manage difficult emotions.

CHAPTER 11:
MENTAL HEALTH
ADVOCACY &
ACTIVISM

Anxiety- a storm in the night sky, that is dark and unrelenting. But just as with all storms, there is a way to channel the energy and that is by engaging in mental health advocacy and activism. Mental health advocacy and activism can be incredibly effective tools for treating anxiety, spreading awareness about mental health issues, and taking part in movements to promote positive change.

Mental health advocacy and activism can be powerful tools for those struggling with anxiety, as it has the power to elevate awareness of mental health issues and amplify the voices of individuals facing challenges. It is also a great way for people to make a meaningful impact on their communities by helping support those in need.

Understanding the Importance of Mental Health Advocacy and Activism

Mental health advocacy and activism are important tools in fighting the stigma surrounding mental disorders such as anxiety and depression. Advocacy is an important way to support those living with mental health conditions by creating awareness and ensuring that adequate resources are available for them. Activism involves taking action to push for change within our communities, whether at a local, state, or federal level.

The importance of raising awareness about mental health issues cannot be overstated. By engaging in conversations and creating dialogue, individuals can help reduce stigma and create an environment that is more accepting of those facing anxiety. Advocacy can involve public speaking, attending rallies or marches, joining organizations that support mental health, writing letters to legislators, etc. These actions allow individuals to make their voices heard and help create positive change in society's perception of mental health issues.

Activism is also a powerful way to bring about real policy changes that can make an impact on individuals' lives. By taking direct action, citizens can push for legislation or regulations that will improve mental health care in the country. Activism can be anything from collecting signatures for petitions to planning and executing protest marches. It is a great way for individuals to show their support for mental health and make an impact on policy decisions that affect them. Ultimately, both advocacy and activism can make a mark by providing a sense of community, empowerment, and purpose to combat these debilitating mental health conditions.

Strategies For Taking Part in Mental Health Activism

We now know that mental health activism is a powerful way to create positive change in society's perceptions and attitudes toward mental health issues. Being an advocate or activist for mental health can be intimidating, but there are several steps that anyone can take to make their voices heard. If you are interested in taking part in mental health advocacy or activism, there are a few strategies that can help you get started.

1.   **Research**: First off, do your research about the issue you are passionate about. Take time to learn more about the causes and organizations involved in this work, as well as any relevant policies or legislation that could help address the issue. It is also important to make sure you are prepared for any potential risks or consequences that may be involved in participating in these activities.

2.   **Share your story**: Sharing your experiences with mental illness can help reduce stigma and raise awareness about the importance of mental health. As *Glennon Doyle*, author of the bestselling memoir "Untamed," notes, "When we share our stories, we connect with others and create a sense of belonging."

3.   **Build connections**: Networking with like-minded individuals who share similar goals is also an important part of being an effective advocate. Networking helps build relationships with people who have similar interests and values and allows them to work together toward a common goal. As a mental health advocate and author of "Reasons to Stay Alive," *Matt Haig* notes, "Activism isn't just about yelling at people; it's about asking for change."

4.   **Support mental health organizations**: Supporting mental health organizations can help fund research, education, and advocacy efforts. This can involve donating money, volunteering your time, or participating in fundraising events. As a mental health advocate and actress *Glenn Close* notes, "We have to support organizations that are working to help people with mental illness."

5.   **Educate yourself and others**: Educating yourself about mental health and sharing that knowledge with others can help reduce stigma and improve understanding. This can involve reading books, watching documentaries, attending workshops, and sharing resources on social media. As author and mental health advocate *Jenny Lawson* notes, "The more we talk about mental health, the less scary it becomes."

6.   **Stay up to date:** Finally, it is important to stay informed on any recent advancements or changes when it comes to mental health policies or treatments that could benefit the public. Staying on top of news stories related to mental health issues or policy changes ensures that advocates are up-to-date on anything that might impact them personally or professionally and allows them to remain active in the cause even if they cannot physically attend events or

rallies.

Whatever your chosen method of advocacy or activism, it is important to remember that every action counts and can make a difference in the lives of those living with anxiety or other mental health issues. Meanwhile, taking care of your mental health is crucial to being an effective mental health activist. As a mental health advocate and author of "The Gifts of Imperfection," *Brené Brown* notes, "Self-care is not selfish; it's necessary for your well-being."

In conclusion, mental health advocacy and activism are powerful tools for combating the stigma surrounding mental illness. By understanding the importance of raising awareness about mental health issues, engaging in meaningful conversations, networking with like-minded individuals, and taking direct action to push for policy changes, anyone can make a positive impact and contribute to a more compassionate and understanding society when it comes to mental health.

FINAL THOUGHTS

Congratulations! You have made it to the end of your journey in healing from anxiety - now you are ready to take flight and soar. Just like a bird that has been learning how to fly, you have gone through the stages of building up strength, understanding what holds you back, and finally spreading your wings with confidence. It's time for you to start living life with newfound freedom and clarity! So let's get started on this exciting new adventure together – one step at a time.

You have learned so much in this book about anxiety and depressive illness – from understanding the anatomy of our emotions and how they affect us, to developing healthy coping mechanisms, to recognizing our triggers and creating an action plan for managing them. Now that you have all these tools in your arsenal, it's time to put them into practice! Here are a few actionable steps you can take to integrate this newfound knowledge into your life:

- Take a few moments each day to pause and reflect on how far you have come on your journey. Celebrate the progress that you have made and give yourself credit for all the hard work and dedication you have put in!

- Make a list of all the healthy coping mechanisms you have learned in this book, and commit to using them whenever you feel anxious.

- Create a support system for yourself – be it friends, family members, or even online communities – so that you know you always have someone to turn to when times get tough.

- Remind yourself that anxiety is a normal emotion and that it's okay to feel it. Self-compassion is key!

- Most importantly, don't be afraid to get back up when you fall down. Everyone has setbacks in life – the important thing is to learn from them and move on.

Remember, no journey is ever easy, but taking that first step is always worth it. We hope that this book has provided you with the tools, motivation, and encouragement to truly begin your journey toward healing from anxiety and depression– and we invite you to continue on this path of self-discovery! As long as you stay curious, kind to yourself, and committed to making positive changes in your life, there is no limit to what you can achieve.

We wish you all the best in your journey toward healing and thank you for taking the time to read this book. Good luck on your path to recovery, you have got this!